SADNESS
&
SHORT BLISS
Plus the undefined

*The debut poetry collection
by*
KYOMI WADE

Composed by Kyomi Wade.
Illustrated & designed by Sinduja Chandrapalan.

Copyright © 2017 Dream Markt Publishing
All rights reserved.
ISBN: 978-1-9998779-0-3

To my mother
As it means to me
It means to you

*

To the writers
And the muses
My musings are you

*

To myself
You did it
Because of those who love you

*

To the reader
For your heart and time
I say, thank you

'The sadness will last forever.'

-Vincent van Gogh

Why Sadness?

It's important to know that this collection wasn't originally created for the purpose of publishing. It was created to let things out, express a feeling or two and because the words from my heart and head seemed to take my burden with them every time they reached a page. So of course, upon trying to present them to the world they were essentially a mish-mash of defining moments in my life, mixing the different voices I had as I grew up. Thus - it was hard to group them together.

What I did notice however was that I tended to write when I was mostly sad – feel free to add a long list of synonyms onto this as I realise this is quite reductive grouping. But when I think of moments of extreme happiness or 'bliss' shall we say, these were the moments in which I rarely thought of my pen, they were often moments so brief, that I sat dazed - staring at them, as they became less clear in the distance and eventually became another memory stored in my mind.

What is happiness anyway? There is much research counteracting the idea that it is a destination, explaining rather, that it is an emotion. My title is a nod to this, as it is similar to my own thoughts about life. That they are filled with random bouts of happiness. All the moments in-between are longing for that feeling again, or anxiety attached to losing it, or simply the overwhelming state of glee that reduces you to living for it - and eventually drives you mad.

Maybe I am describing love, but as we know, the two are so intrinsically linked so it is easy to sometimes blur the lines. So perhaps, in many ways this is a book about love. That scary, all consuming thing that painfully forces our steps but also makes the world go round.

You may find that as a reader, you question some of the placements in the *Short Bliss* chapter, and you would not be wrong to do so. Many times they are served with other emotions, or bittersweet. In fact, I'm of the belief that the only poem within this collection that champions untainted happiness is *Your Love*, a poem I wrote for one of my dearest friends who was getting married at the time.

The Untitled are emotions I could not quite assign, a sort of: I don't even know how I feel anymore. The other side of sadness, definitely not 'happiness', not fear, not anger, none of the basic emotions that we know. I found most of these were acceptance, observation poetry, or indeed a struggling assessment of how I was feeling, as I couldn't quite place it.

It's been a tumultuous and wonderful experience to unearth these poems from my phone, laptop and faded notebooks. Shelved emotions have awoken angry, demanding that they re-enter my mind;

I have had to patiently return them to my subconscious, scared that they might again want to be felt by their owner.

I am glad they are now safe, in the sense that they won't be lost, as many words have been before. They are documented. They are sure. They are very real and they are mini-saviours. As I release my words into the metaphorical air I bid them farewell with my heart in my mouth, hoping that they are understood.

I hope you, the reader, may connect with the things I say. I hope that if you feel the way I've felt, you know that I understand you, as many poets have kindly done to me. But mostly I hope, that at least for you, the sadness does not last forever.

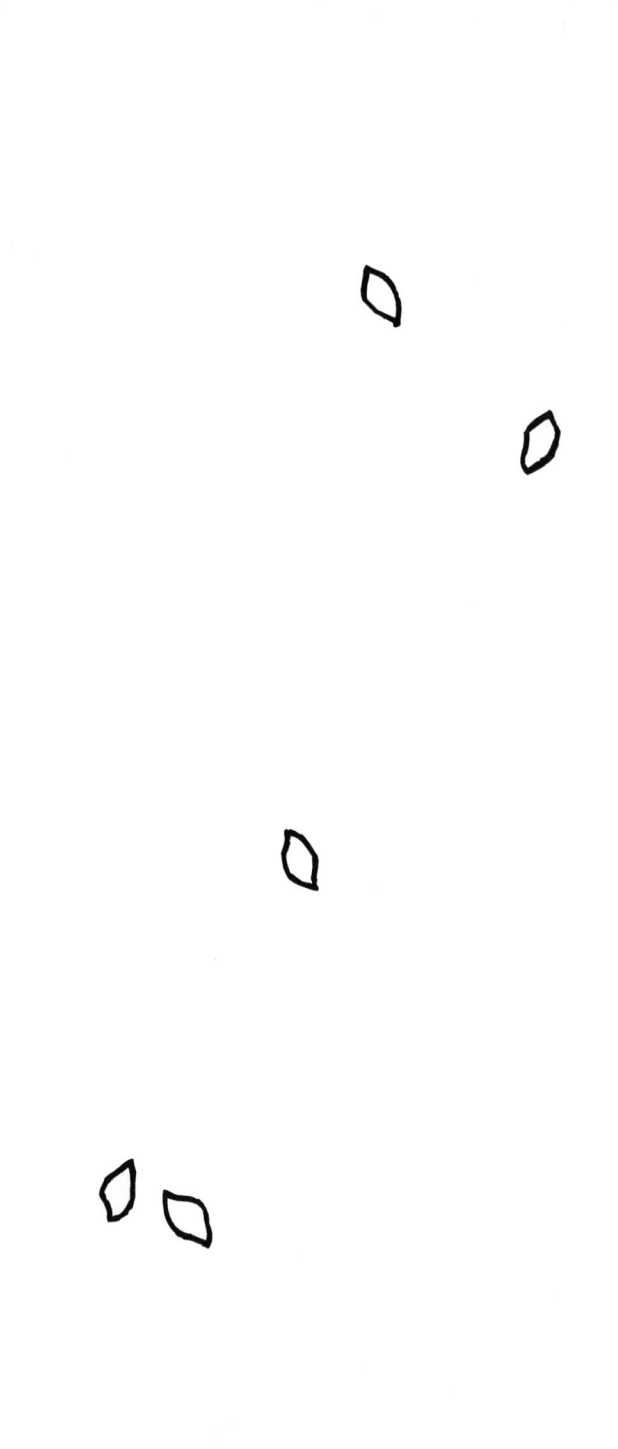

SADNESS

A non-starter morning	1
Powerless	3
Nobody home	5
Empty	6
The thoughts that shake you/the love that makes you	7
The Weakness in She	9
An appeal to time	10
There's no answer, sweetheart	13
A letter to myself	15
Comfort in numbers?	17
Bungee Jumping	18
Mind Meditation	19
The heart and time	23
Business is closed	25
The big bang	27
Pain is acute, especially in the dark	29
My baby	30
Thoughts for an old friend	31
A midnight plea	32
I may begin new consuming	33
Playing with fire	35
Loser	37
A bonus essay: love and other thoughts	39

SHORT BLISS

Light	43
The complication of feelings	45
Plantito	46
A nothing manifesto	47
Communication	49
With me, no choice	51
Bask, with caution	53
Love, on a good day	54
The Soul Dance	55
Your love	57
I saw you	59
Love	61
A reminder	62

THE UNDEFINED

Go and clean your room!	65
A slice of life	67
A tale of the Great Nan	69
Let me make sweet music with my sister	71
Out of Line	72
Offering the insides	73
Survival of the Fittest	74
The Fairytale?	75
A London Li(f)e Desired	76
Westminster: an apology to London	77
Grenfell	79
Dual-weather	81
I learned of a city	83
The hand that pulls you	85
In These Streets	86
Life has no stillness	87
My Mind is Spread	89
The chaos of longing (K.Y. Robinson)	91
Motions and potions	92
Healing	93
Thank you	98
Bonus Poem	99

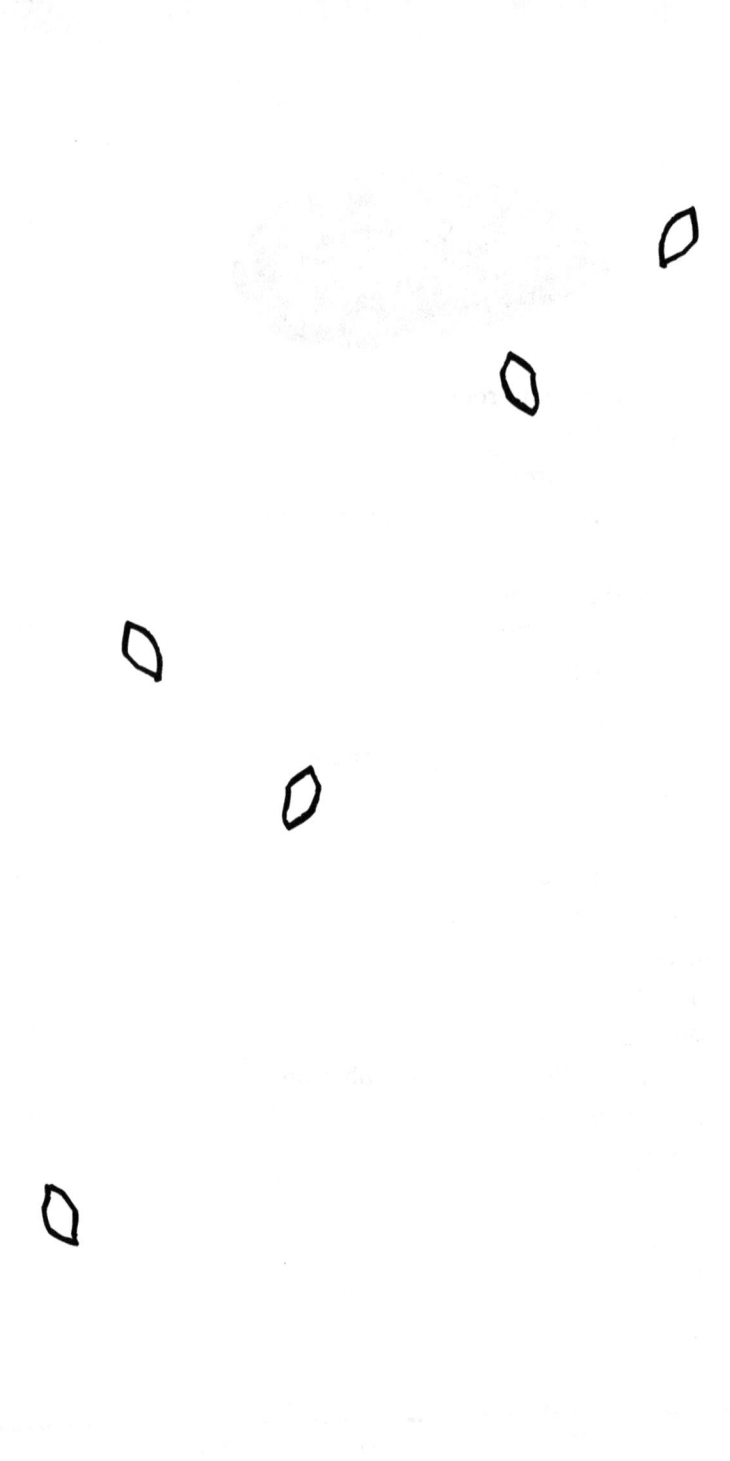

SADNESS

A non-starter morning

The day felt heavy at its start. Journeying until the end was hard to picture.

Far far far away, a cold place, with no comfort but the promise of the blanket night ready to soothe with darkness and blank pictures.

Fast-forward me to then.

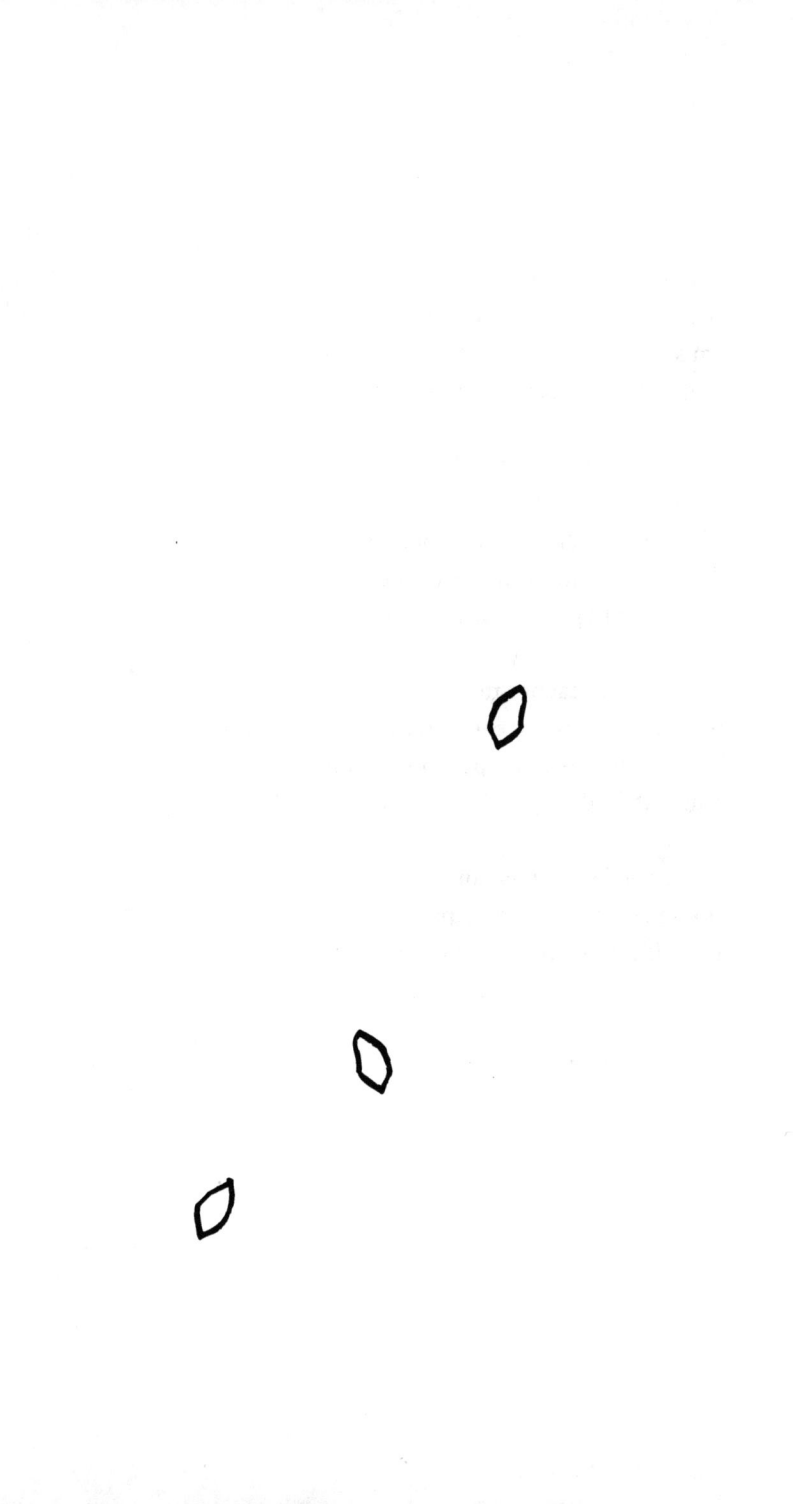

Powerless

In that misty murky sphere
I'm sure that demons chase you
I'm sure they hide in pitch-black pockets
Camouflaging beneath the purple clouds

Too murky for light to live there?
I wonder if it ever clears
The smiling shield had protected the rest
While you withered in a corner,
and the cold pierced your chest

And now it reaches me in my breath
Wasted, as you retreat into the dark expanse
I called on love and upon it clenched
You watched me, rocking forth and back

In the swirls of angst and fear
Does my love not enter past the ear?
The blackness blocks and fills the air
From vision, from touch

I lost you there.

Nobody home

Today if you speak to me you will get words only
My soul is hidden in some dark corner
Of a room in my mind

I think of, but cannot feel her anymore
And that is too painful for me to conceal
Where has she disappeared, this time?

I know the words you're supposed to say
The things you're supposed to do
To get by – look alive
I can do that, I can speak - I would sleep
But I don't feel it either

I don't feel you; physically, emotionally
I cannot feel you today
Please don't approach me I have nothing to say

Perhaps a hole that will eclipse you
As I get lost - don't let me grip you
Just walk the other way
And find some new joy/ some new life

Find a smile, a warm reception
Grab what you can get that thrills you
Even better if it fills you
But consider me empty

Empty

first love… then stillness
so many windy hours pass by

i hold my head still

the air whips
me and stings occasionally

The thoughts that shake you / the love that makes you

When I loved you you were only you. Free to stretch and hold me between your fingers not bound by wires behind your back, tied to responsibility or the heart of another / I could never love another, so heavy, adorned with complication and wracked with the wretchedness of life in his heart, in his face / the feeling is engraved, the feeling passes pain, the cold is your friend, I know it / on your face, in the frowns there are deep crevices of emptiness, where you wonder where you've gone and who you are. I just want to hold you because I know.

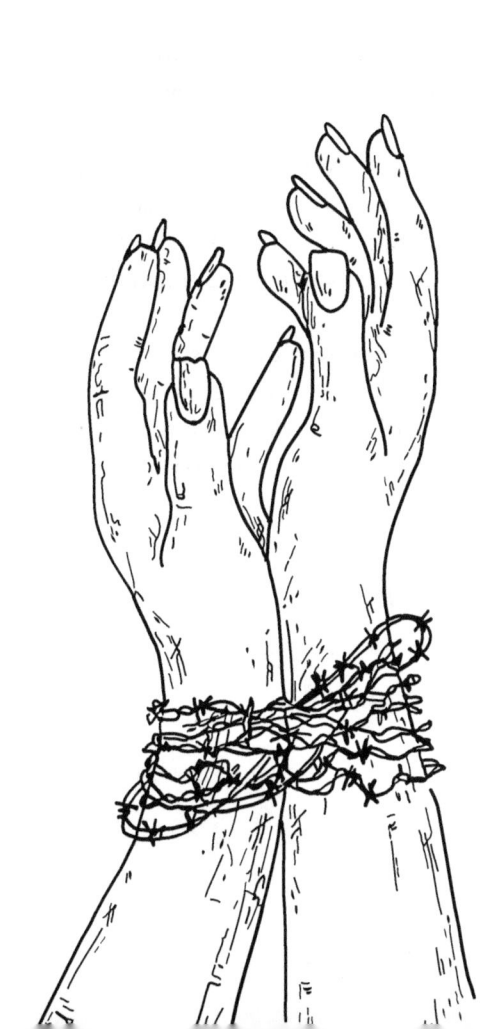

The Weakness in She

Limping, stuttering, barely breathing
Deafened, numb and partially seeing
Handshake weak, and eyes that wander
Spine so soft, thus inevitable slumber

And watch there the fool, quietly watching
Convinced that there lies the iron bars of her path
A star could not lead her to any dwellings of the wise
Hellish burns could not loosen the tightness of her grasp

She prayed for walls, the ground and a ceiling
She prayed for a force to harness the feeling
She prayed for motivation to move towards the light
She prayed for someone to finish the fight

She watched intently as he stumbled in stride
Convincing herself of a reason to lie
Underneath the covers, in darkness and blind
She silently prayed for an eternal night

An appeal to time

Love burns strong
Where is on?
That place I'm blindly moving

Not fools' time, nor of mine
But I am tired of searching

If I am many and you are mighty
Then why not lead the way?

Let me go to the peace-land
Let me go because you can

"Self sabotage hath looked much finer"

There's no answer, sweetheart

Restless and older
I ponder a resolution
The promise of a resolution
Is a young heart's dream

A letter to myself

So many meanings
So many words
So many lines
Typed to you

Typing...
Writing
Typing...
Then silence

And you?
Frantic
Answering the statements
Shaking up conclusions
Giving arguments
New hope

But, do you know?
It won't work
So every letter is
Wasted: energy, seconds
You could be healing

So try, my darling
Lay back on your pillow
Let it carry
And harness
Your pain for the night

Rest your will
Rest your fingers
Rest your words
Rest those feelings
Let this fluffy promise
Awake you kindly to light

When the morning comes
And you've dreamed your sums
Take both hands, and do not grab
Your phone - grab life

Comfort in numbers

Love is so beautiful, but life, so rough
The natural, painful, peak and trough
Sometimes in company, others the worst - alone
And as it goes and goes, driving madness to each one

Bungee Jumping

For all the muster and bravery
Of a heart
The stillness is almost a comfort
The loss from each and every direction
Is final but so sudden
I'm falling-
Apart, the pieces lie dead like shrapnel
Grasping is useless and hurtful
I smile and remember the fire
As it burned in my eyes
And not inside me

Mind Meditation

When the worry scatters like atoms
In a sphere unseen and unknown
Undetectable to the ignorant eye
They claim 'the open ones'

Your mind is on a trip
Back, a painful place
One that makes you shut your eyes
But refuses to go away

And even worse when it reaches the future
The cause, effect, the fate
Fake smile whilst your mind is ticking
A slow and painful wait

But when that thought is sometimes pleasure
You might dwell within its air
For longer, warmer and dream like
You lose track of how long you've been there

And they say dwell as if you were a haunting
Trespasser or unpleasant smell
They term you this, almost as if
It wasn't your own hearts story to tell

They expect a spiteful jolt as you travel forward
Conscious, through the mind-spell

Then, now and in due time
They turn in the circle of my mind

The perfect past is so divine
Surely its existence is enough for I
Love to occasionally bask in its beams
And let the tear-drops dry

"I know we both can't feel the same thing at the same time"

The heart and time

There is no soothing
For the fresh wound of a hearts cry
As it pines and pains
At mercy to time

And watch how time strolls
Mocking as passing
Singing to the time-old melody
Played out by my heart strings

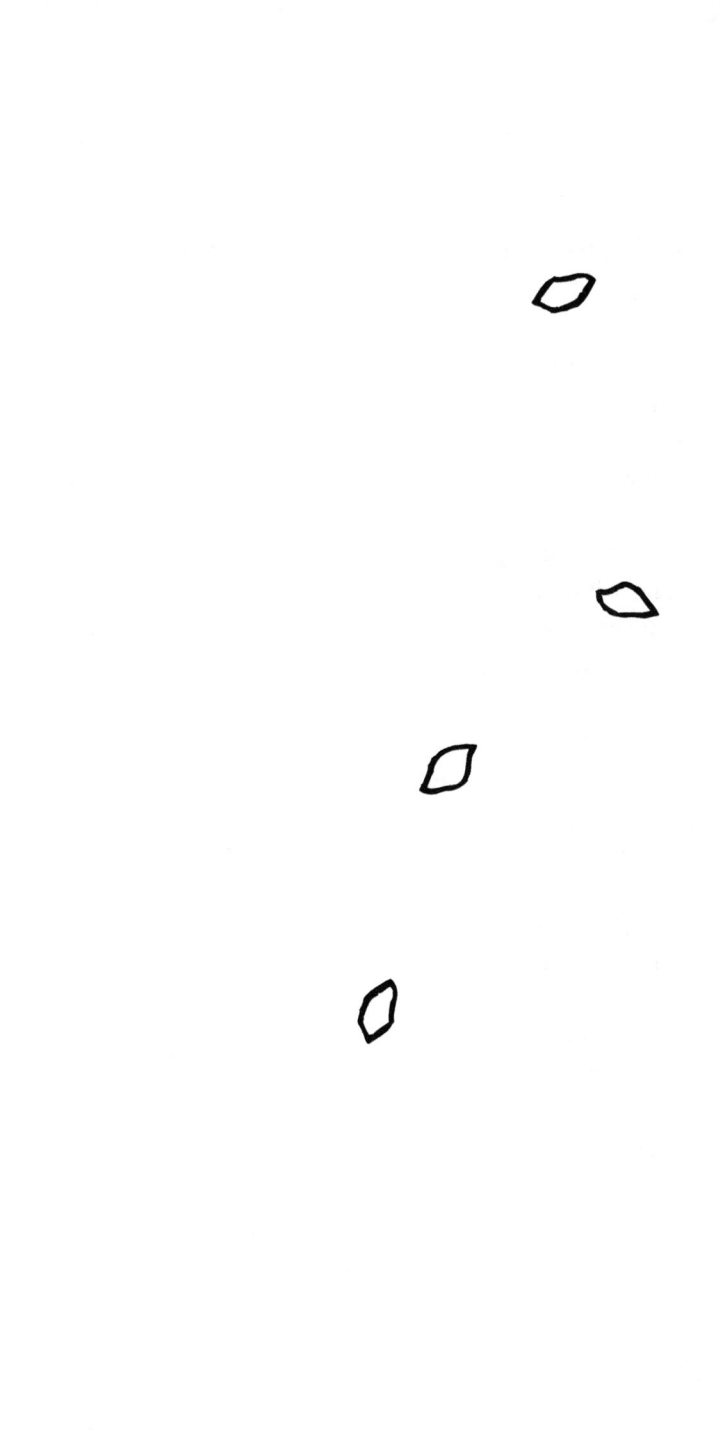

Business is closed

it's a dreadful training process undoing the heart's work
drying up sentiments and turning it to stone

but now i know i can't
and i've promise that i shan't
the lessons ensue
and it has to be so

we know the story of the flower
and how it tilts towards the sun
but never spoke of the power
when the sun did shun

each petal must close one by one
each need must turn into want

because now i know i can't
and i've promised that i shan't
i am blind, to its shine
and it has to be so

we know the story of the magnet
of the north and the south
destined to be as one
forever bound

this pole must travel very far
so the magic call is as distant as the stars

because now i know i can't
and i've promised that i shan't
i must be out of reach
and it has to be so

we all know the story of the thing
that thinks it can fly
spread its arms
and touch the sky

it must stay on the ground and never think high
it must look down not lustfully, at the sky

because now i know i can't
and i've promised that i shan't
i'll have grounded dreams
and it has to be so

and until time sees it just
feel i must
my heart will be breaking
but i must not show!

The big bang

It always hits with grandeur
Knowing you care
Waking the hearts' anguish from dusty sleep
By some minor-tragic affair

It always catches you at the darkest hours
What it is you feel
Funny how the dark
Tells us of light, and what's real

It always hits you in the silence
When there's no one to tell the lies to
The heart will scream loudest
Only audible to you

It always chips away at the soul
Wondering, if it is – mutual
Worst yet, is the tantalising hope
That you might just say, me too

Pain is acute, especially in the dark

In the darkness of the evening

Positivity is an old and uncool friend / unwelcomed, uninformed, undressed and exposed / to let judgment form / the sadness pulls it all: face, arms, legs, down / and / as I drag my feet down, this too long road / I feel myself dripping / letting it touch the floor and the arms, of the people who pass

In the darkness of the evening

Love is someone I do not know / hostility lasts / the darkness brings pain with sharpness / I feel myself slipping – letting go of a loose handle / not fit for the weight of my soul

In the darkness of the evening

A smile is something I cannot find / pleasantry is frozen / coal and cold air is hard to take in / but I don't feel it / the blanket of black the night soothes, the grooves get deeper, but the beloved night conceals it

My Baby

Do you know the sound
Of a parent
Who has lost their child?
It escaped from my mouth
And the people thought
I had lost
My baby

In a way
I had

Thoughts for an old friend

I saw it was your son's birthday today
Online, as always, with news these days
My heart sank low, how time had flown
We had not met - yet I called myself a good friend

It is likely you are full, content and in peace
These are words kind Comfort says to me
Surely your days are the fairest they have been
With a sun as your son, and a beautiful queen

You are grateful, forgiving and oh so wise
So I know, could maybe bet, that you would say, "it's fine"
"It's life, I'm well, are you?" And I'd respond
But know I miss greatly our friendship and bond

Life rolls on, chapters close
And perhaps it is just 'one of those'
But dear old friend, in the silence know
That I wish you the happiest days I've known

A midnight plea

Oh brave new day
Awake me in every way
Make me hold
Each hour
In the palm of my hand
Like a diamond
Gifted by a friend

I may begin new consuming

I may begin new consuming
I'm afraid of what I have learnt
Not purposely but worldly
I am spoken for, and weary

I shake my head
So slowly, it's heavy
The dust moves as an avalanche
From the branches of my mind

I am saddened by my state
Stationary, waiting for some magical liqueur
To wake me from my society slumber

If I were to take a line from a sonnet
It may be the sweetest I have plenty seen
I would pray that the richness stayed in my soul
And not only in my dreams

Playing with fire

It's the match that strikes against the matchbox
When you know you just know
Like the nature of fire
That grows and grows

Beginning was end
Friend was pretend
Something was spent
And it goes and goes

Unfair, destructive, inconsolable, uncontrollable
It burns still – unstoppable
As if it doesn't know

The end is nigh, the fall is high
Bold and blind movements
But life had told!

It's a shame, they should have never
Ever ever, struck together
And now neither is better
And the creases are wetter

And the damage cuts the soul
And some don't let go
Bringing wood to the fire
As it grows and grows

Loser

Even in my dreams I lose you
I forget the colours of your cheeks
Ever creating with my weary pen
You are the ink it leaks

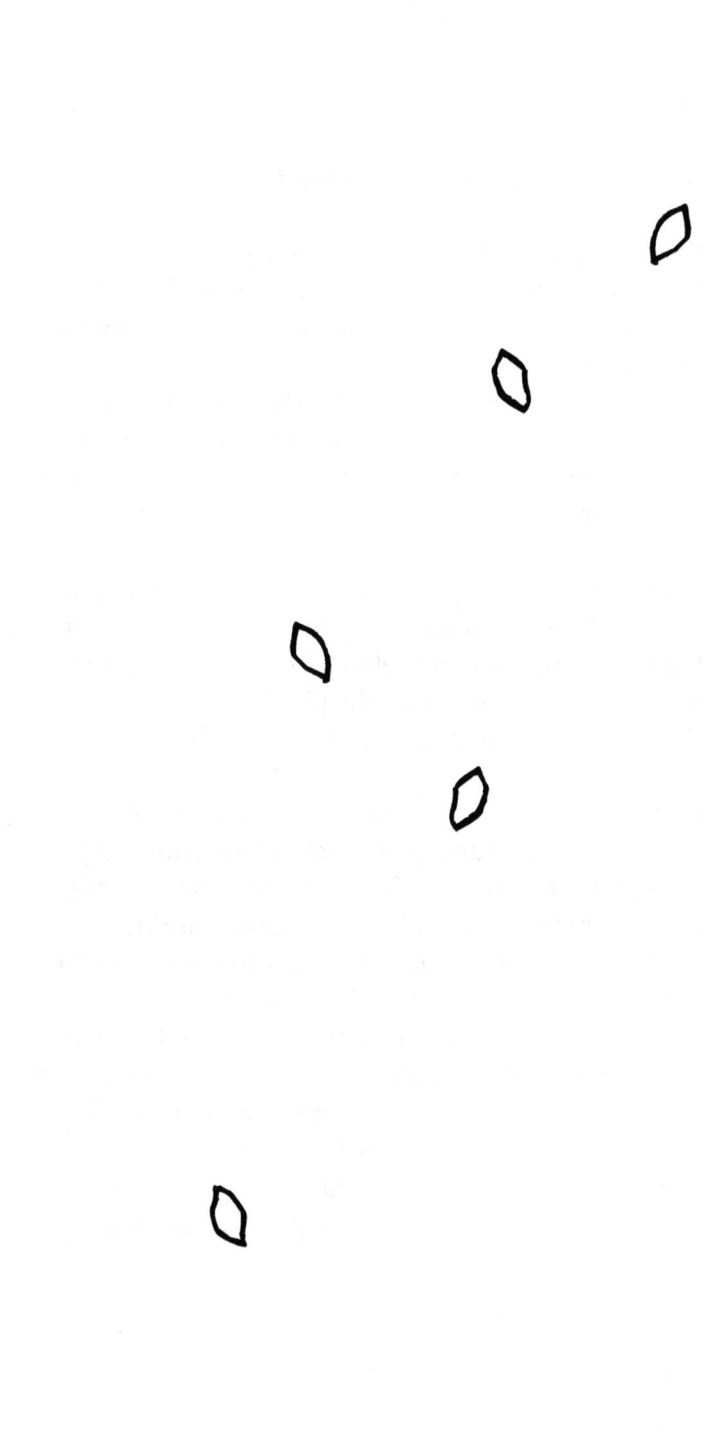

A bonus essay: love and other thoughts

I was tempted to be overwhelmed by my unshakable love for someone, who walked nonchalantly through the chapters of my mind, who danced in my dreams and treaded over new memories. And who now, brought surprising tears to my face that truly seemed to come from deep in my subconscious, triggered by a well-written love story that apparently was offering me catharsis, as I naively buried myself in its pages.

I remembered that life wasn't so spiteful, that it grants us all dashed-hopes and personal horrors, that pulls the smiles from your cheeks and clears your eyes to see things that slowly pull the pit of your stomach to the floor, and you walk a little less upright for it.

I acknowledged the intensity of my thoughts for my love of him, and thought of clichés concerning my now partner. A woman who may have loved her self less may have said I don't deserve him, but this didn't seem like the right allocation. I was sure we were all living with things that killed us daily. The life you live without the type of love that grips you firmly and dashes you in front of the mirror to face your eclipsed eyes and throbbing heart is merely an existence. But eventually that day you pray for greets you subtly, and you are eased back into life, the colour returns to your cheeks and you believe too that you are restored.

Until, in a moment of euphoria, you realise that you once felt a deeper happiness; that the peak of your contentment lies behind every coming-moment in the timeline of your life.

And how cruel, that these moments occupy the smallest chapters of our life? That we are not prepared, as we are by our carers, who whether it is with all the stationery in the world, or even just the correct shirt, send us to school with some tools to learn. But with love you are often blind-sighted, and no one teaches you how to keep living while the heart protests and confesses its sins daily. Or how, in the silence of the truth to hide its loud and deliberate twists and turns. It is a testing process that breaks many, dulls the rest and immobilises the last to live with bitterness and salty tears that are eternally hidden from the world.

I, had moved from the first option to the second, and had accepted that my days would be shadowed by a subtle sadness that told me love had missed me. I had received a drop by accident, when love was watering the fields. And although I looked up, longingly, waiting to receive more, I was slowly realising that nothing was coming. Life had served me, and I would go to sleep with a rumbling stomach tonight.

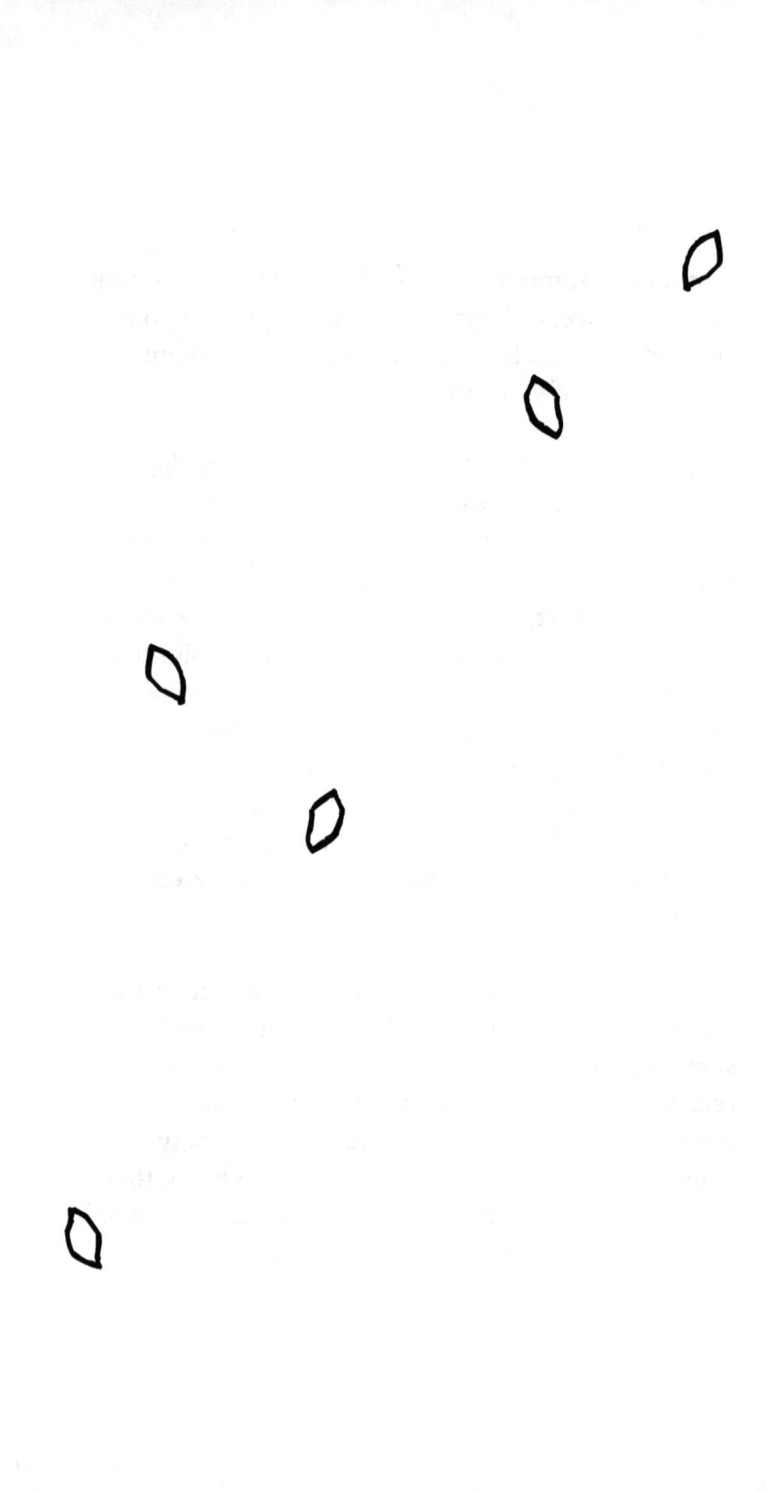

SHORT BLISS

Light

In the messiness of my mind
There is the window in the corner
There is brightness between its squares
It is a blue so divine

Why condense such happiness?
So small I thought it not reality
A hiccup in my brain I cannot touch
It is the window to my dreams

The complication of feelings

Oh tell me what it is to feel for another
A trap, an attack, a test, I wonder
All guilty, all affected, all attested to this number
A time old tale worth timeless humour

And you sit there, apparently your own human being
Waiting on affirmation from another human being
And if within that time, one could compare your heart to ice
Even the smallest acknowledgement
Turns that ice, to ice cream

And that ice cream drips down, down to the cone
You are solid in nothing – which makes you resolve
"Tis better not to have, than to melt your being
And to crave that which is out of your control"

But now, please admire how he holds me so
My gaze, my waist, my attention is whole
Discard my thoughts, my thoughts are him
So much for intentions and words, I am a human being

Plantito

For endless days she regarded him, like a flower
She watered him just enough to survive

Gazed, smelled the sweet fragrance
But never close enough
To touch – not enough - to feel the prickly leaves

It was to be so
Staring from a glass-home

Except she longed to hold the stem
And lightly brush the petals with her fingers

A nothing manifesto

To feel nothing at all is a blessing
It's my quiet, it's my bliss
No longer do evil soldiers walk through my trodden mind
You see nothing is kind

Nothing allows me to dream loosely
Non-committed and green in intention
What I have seen can no longer blind me
You see nothing is my redemption

To live peacefully without connection
Is my Oasis and contentment
Expectation, emotion and resentment free
Is the state teasing, calling, pulling me

Time must be shorted
Handshakes weaker
Embraces are further
Kisses fleeting
Empathy distanced
Do not rely
Do not feel the urgency
To reply
Love must be isolated
Put in boxes
Do not play
This never-ending race
You must be still
Do not affect

Do not trample
Quietly respect
Love be in the heart
But pray, stay there
If nothing is property
No loss, or despair

If you can master this beautiful art
Tensions can release and friendship, eternal
You are not losing your weary-battle heart
Just ensuring no hurt and not being hurtful

Communication

How I love, my special one
When sentences dance between our tongues
As soon as you start, I speak it done
As soon as we part, both rendered dumb

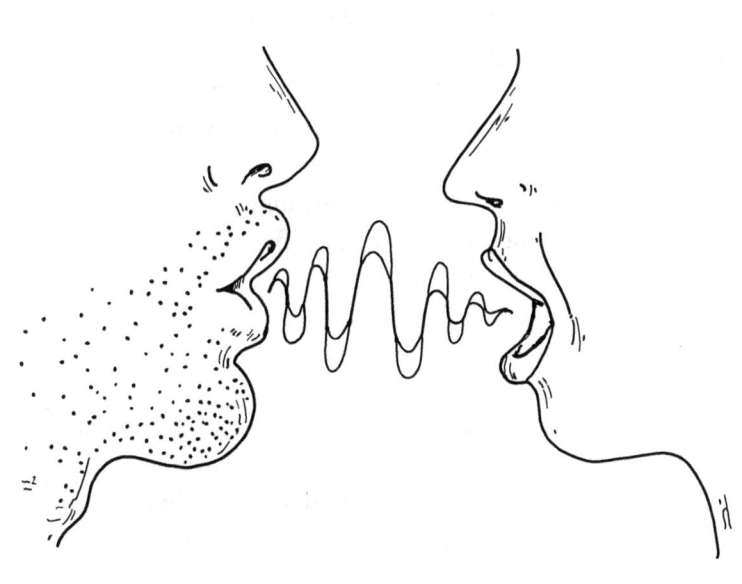

With me, no choice

When I look up at you I am sure of nothing
but that I don't want to look away.

Your hands firmly charge me for
Journeying on these mundane streets
Your smell transports me to scenes of beauty
And a cocoon of safeness

Can I bear it, or might it twist me into madness?
Like the mile deep grooves that paint these trees
How unshakable, this feeling that turns me, disturbs me
Like the sun that beats down on my exposed skin

When I welcome it in, it heats up my limbs
So that life is a dance, I grow with my flames
Take me to the saddest hour!
Take me to the darkest street!
I illuminate my settings, in every shade

When I shun, it turns violent, moving slowly inside of me
Like a low burning fire, the smoke smiles sadistically
Choking to eventual silence, it is with me perpetually
This feeling is a poison, but it seems my wants precede me

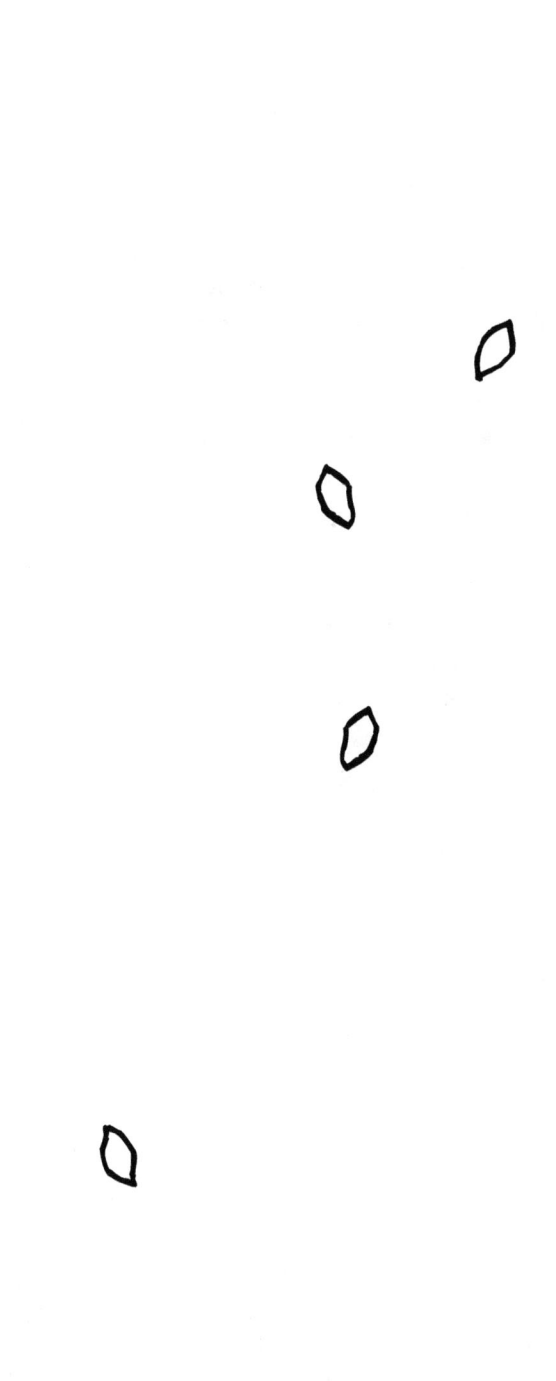

Bask, with caution

I saw you open the door today
I saw how you let it shine on your face
Love, my love did dance around you and overwhelm you
All smiles, I glow for this seemingly impossible moment

But I fear for you, love. My love is not enough
To protect you from hurt, the world is so harsh
Though my love is ripe and warm, darkness does seep,
I know of the creaks and we are permeable to pain

With my aged love still, life holds you hostage in your soul
And though, you now bask, I pray you don't answer its call
I don't think you know, what lies beneath you
It is a great, and I fear fatal, fall

Love, on a good day

Love love love is all around.
I have it to give
Where needs it?

Here it is to touch your shoulder, you are not lonely
Here it is to listen and understand, you are heard
Here it is to bring laughter to your soul
And your lips, energise them

Tell me where else needs my leaking light?
Let me lead the way with gladness
Let me dry those wet cheeks of sadness, with touch
Hold on when it is all too much

You will not die despite this unbearable walk
In brash mornings mourning remains but so does breath
It is life; we must stroll on, so to me, you can rely
I will ache with your ache, I will cry with your cry

I will smile away your pain, I will hug numb-pain sharp
Let me love you as you emerge begrudgingly from the dark

The Soul Dance

Poetry and your eyes
Make my soul
Dance, like no one is watching
My body? That cage.
I'm afraid
That's another story

Your love (wedding poem)

Katie and James
Your love follows you always
Through to your core and through your eyes -
so you see the world differently

It goes on through to us as we gaze through our wet eyes
That you may both be yourselves,
and each other at the same time

Your union is admiration
And we all see it clear
James, your happy home
Katie, your hero

Keeping life light with laughter
When the darkness floods in
You both are precious lights
To each other, and to us

We see it
We feel it
It dances in the air
To some dub-reggae song
Anything else would be wrong
It pulses through our hearts
And we'll take it with us to dance
James and Kate
Your love is great

Steady and unwavering
A giver of calm
A keeper of youth
A keeper of you
A bubble of happy
A place of safe
A home for the good times
And eternal motivation

Protect and provide
In you James personified
Caring and bubbly
In you my dear Katie

Surely the best lightbulb you have ever received
To decide to live your life
With your love
Eternally

And as for us
We have the pleasure of seeing you today
And then we have the honour to support you, always

As two
As one
As you grow
Because we know
That all in life must end
But your love, never so!

I saw you

I saw you when you were
Only you
Untainted and soul-facing
You were a remarkable thing
Glistening, come morning
Or night

You gave me reason to gaze
I think now those were my best spent days

Love

Through misty-eyed vision, my thoughts are not blurred
I still believe in you
Though I may lie unconscious from what has occurred
To keep beating my heart does need to

I close my eyes and dream of a life
Warm colours, blues do falter
But even roses from my dream - make me bleed
And his voice echoes even louder

He still lives in my mind, and this I find
Very close to torture
But you see my lips are waiting to smile
Because I've seen the bigger picture

And although the pains are sharp and deep
Simultaneously you comfort me
Because I know next time you come,
you're coming for keeps

I still believe, Love.

A reminder

You can't simply run into the fire
Look at all these beautiful ropes
Holding your body
Pulling back your limbs
You want to run
Feel the other side of the heat
But it's not all about you -
And therein lies the beauty

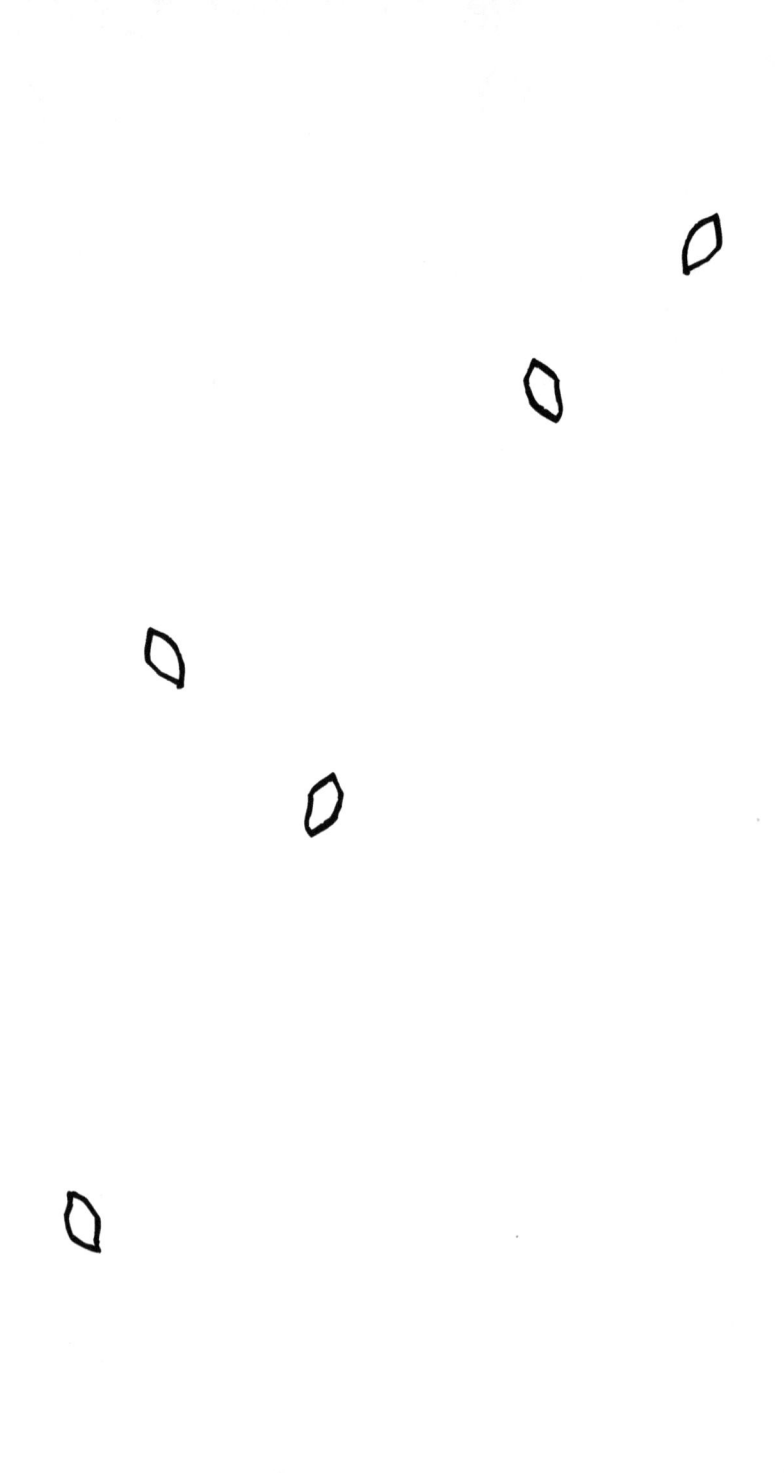

THE UNDEFINED

Go and clean your room!

When everything else is crumbling
Go and clean your room.

Smooth out the creases of the linen
Put all the loose ends in boxes
Sweep the past from your rug
And dust those stable tables

When your cup of tea spills on the rug
Because you vigorously
Scrubbed, don't you give up
Just bleach it away

What I need to tell you
Is that these walls won't clean themselves
Neither will those shelves
So you'll have to speak it with your hands

Tell them what lies after
Make them understand
That if you polish this palace-in-the-making
Life could be grand

If you shut the door you could be
In an alternative world
Where every thing is fine
You are on time

And see they never told you
If you slept through life
You wouldn't have to deal with the mornings
Or the nights

Keep your head above the water
Get your head out of the clouds
But it's fine if you drown
In wine, like they like

And naturally, within your room
No one is ever the wiser
In these walls the world is yours
So more dust, or more shine?

A slice of life

When I was in your kitchen
You monthly-begged me
Child, please
Mind your fingers!

Knife twice the size of
My clambering hands
Powerful in determination
But weak in knowing

While you worried I wondered
How much fear can a mother create?
Always anticipating
Things that never happened

Now I am in my kitchen
And I ponder the deep gash in my hand
I'm worry-wondering if I am
Going numb

And the blood is dripping
But the pain is less
Than your love that sweetly says
I told you to be careful

The tale of the Great Nan

I hope you're not up their fretting
About us you've left behind
When the dust settles on our raw hearts
We'll keep your lessons in our minds

The kindness that you taught us
The fact you never judged us
The keeper of our secrets
The strength in which you loved us

And if I close my eyes
And then open my heart
I feel the softness of your couch
And the love in your smile

You offering me a drink
Or asking if I'm hungry
If I listen really hard
I hear Corry playing faintly

I hope to keep your spirit
In my life, in my words
And I hope to keep your voice
Warm within my heart

I have to say I'm quite grateful
For the memories and the times
If I can still remember your jokes
I can smile and there is hope

****

How can I make you understand,
the greatness of my Nan?
Secret keeper, joy giver and eternal heart winner
I write this little note just to try to explain
The joys and blessings that she gave

Let me make sweet music with my sister

Let me make sweet music with my sister
She feels it all, every single beat

Every tap of instrument
Every bass too low
Every vibration on her skin
Every note within her heart

All the feelings are beating
Every impression - lasting
The music is always playing within
Hear it if you put your ear to the skin

Everything she plays is classic
Everything's in time and magic
And she plays no show or empty tricks
She just breathes out her music

If you skip her melodies, I understand
You listened from your mind instead
You're breaking my heart, so won't you go?
Leave me and my sister alone

Why won't anyone listen to my sister?
She's been leaking that gold
For long, so long

Let me make sweet music with my sister
She plays it so well, that life song

Out of Line

Loyalty to a world capped with regulation; offered support and taught, a system unquestioned.

The lifelong follower foolishly forgotten, unrewarded, undermined, now contemplates disaster.

Eyes eclipsed, sharp fists, loose tongue: sans master.

Offering the insides

They asked for escapism, you gave them the truth
What's the matter with you?
They wanted to dance in delusion
Don't be so harsh with the lights again, so soon

When people long to read between the lines
There's no use offering up your insides on the page like
cold dinner, it's hard to stomach on sunny days
Even less so on a British ones

Maybe I am alone in my thinking
Maybe the thinking-accumulation will rid me of glee
And, perhaps, just perhaps, I'll lose me one day
What separates the mind from sanity anyway?

Survival of the Fittest

A fusion of confusion, a wild attraction
The enigmatic, living, breathing destruction
Thousands of hands working hastily-
Sweat
Talking to themselves: psychological bets
Revlon revolver, black Kohl,
Lipstick and Mac, prepare to blow:
Barry M's in tact
Look on the pack
The sun rises and sets
While the paints still wet

The Fairytale?

It is clear to me that we have been admiring a painting through rose tinted glasses. Primary strokes subject to universal stare are bound to cause speculation. And here's my two-cents: without the glasses I see the secondary strokes / weak and fading colours and the smallest of detail / pain outside the line, dirty blobs and specs of murky colours / the red faded into black and the yellow faded into blue and I ask myself how could I not notice that before? / this painting of crowded overlapping complication of which I prayed to be simple, forgetting that life isn't, was always here / but, sometimes we want it in black and white - it's comforting / that's why I love the expanse of nature / the sky, the trees, the ground, the sun and the moon. I can trust every movement if any, will be smooth / so as the wind gently breathes on my hair. Like a mirror reflection, a similar action on the leaves / and we both breathe / I thank the moon and sun for taking me as their own / and calmly watching as I safely reach home / back to the wall which I hung the canvas on / shaking my head knowing it all so wrong

A London Li(f)e Desired

London tonight
It moves with the mood
Changing like the loose emotions of a London crowd.

Life is choppy
But you must not crumble, only stumble –
Then say it was the fickle wind.

Lie like us
While the truth sinks to the water bed
Pretend like you don't see ripples in the water.

Lie like us
In the words that you sound
You're proud; you've mastered the London style.

Westminster: an apology to London

How many times have I spoke poor of my city?
Forgetting it held the ones I love
Death brings fairness not,
but a message in a blood red postbox
Life is as short as our summer months.

Grenfell

I can't close my eyes

underneath the cloak of tragedy / I am hesitant to touch the scabs of solemn, it's raw, still / If we are brave enough, we might, allow ourselves to absorb the fear of knowing / you're leaving in the cruelest way, your heart, your lungs stretched / out of your body into the bodies around you but still / safety, the grateful breath of air only millimeters away but impossible / and as life is fading away, the 10th floor, a saving grace - in the arms of a man, who knew he could not fail / a human, a baby, it was a girl, a present / a parent, who took a leap no one ever wants to imagine / here's hoping she had one moment of comfort / like the baby, my heart leaps every sound bite, every post, every article, every status, every eye witness quote.

and yet, I still see us twiddling with life between our fingers, looking into the distance / and putting it to the side / we will never know what it's like to grasp it / for air / how could we ever feel it

from the distance of a living room chair?

Dual-weather

I can only blame Emerson for my current view of the sky:
The divine abode of God had the trees subtly sketched
onto it so that when I prayed the trees lightly swayed its
branches and I felt my prayers surround me, as if in some
sort of sending process.

The white scar of Ahab ran across the sky, contrasting
scenes. The left side devoted itself to dark grey clouds,
which were roughly scribbled onto the dusty backdrop.
The second, had the pleasure of the sun, which shined its
light as if it were clearing the dark ones, and so only few
rested at the bottom of the picture.

A conclusion? Some bi-polar reflection of a familiar mood,
Two paths that the sky did truly allude.

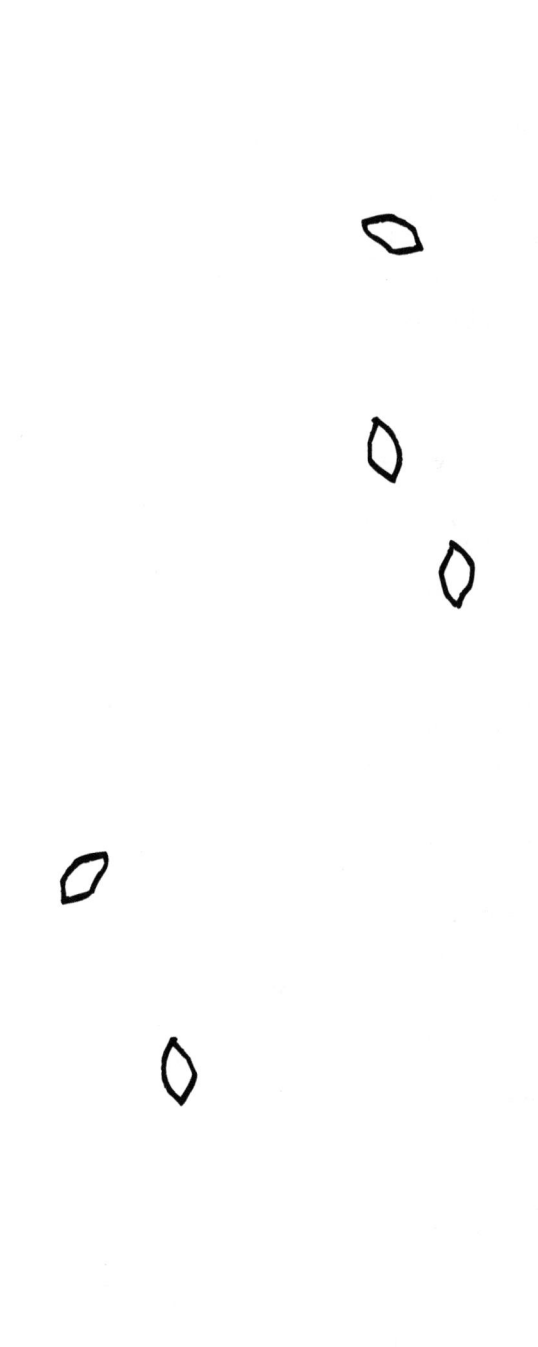

I learned of a city

I learned of a city
Through you
Every street told
Me more - I wanted

When I trace
My steps
I find parts of you

If not a smile
A moment
Eternalised
On a corner

I learned of a city
So long ago

Something lived
Is still
and distant

I think rosy of
This place
In the details
Your face

So casual
I forget to
Separate it

I learned of a city
In thick books

Great people
brave souls
I could taste it
In the air

And yes
I told stories
of its magic
Its charm

But it seems
it was you
You were always
there

The hand that pulls you

A stranger, a man, with a knowing smile
Talks through the motions of the dancing that ensues
And while many lines of the poem are unwritten
A quiet confidence foresees scenes true

Am I so subservient that I follow this path?
Am I unable to cause direction?
Am I a nervous creator with no faith in my own?
Do I, reduce I, while I silently follow?

Life is rolling
Resolve is strolling
I loosely hang on.
And where are the convictions that hold me strong?

In These Streets

Like a fly
He is moving
Disappearing
Over heads
Swirling
Between ears
Buzzing
Phone in pocket
You can hear
But never see
'Cause he's dancing
Full speed
And he'll keep on
Buzzing
'Till the day
Someone swats him

Life has no stillness

There is a rush to every moment
That never seems to slow
A hurry to all the days
I never care to know

A brush past all the seconds
I prayed to slow
I was at his doorstep
I was asked to go

I am rushing back
To something I know
I'm running around
It's quite a show

All that excitement
Watch me go!
Chasing what?
I do not know

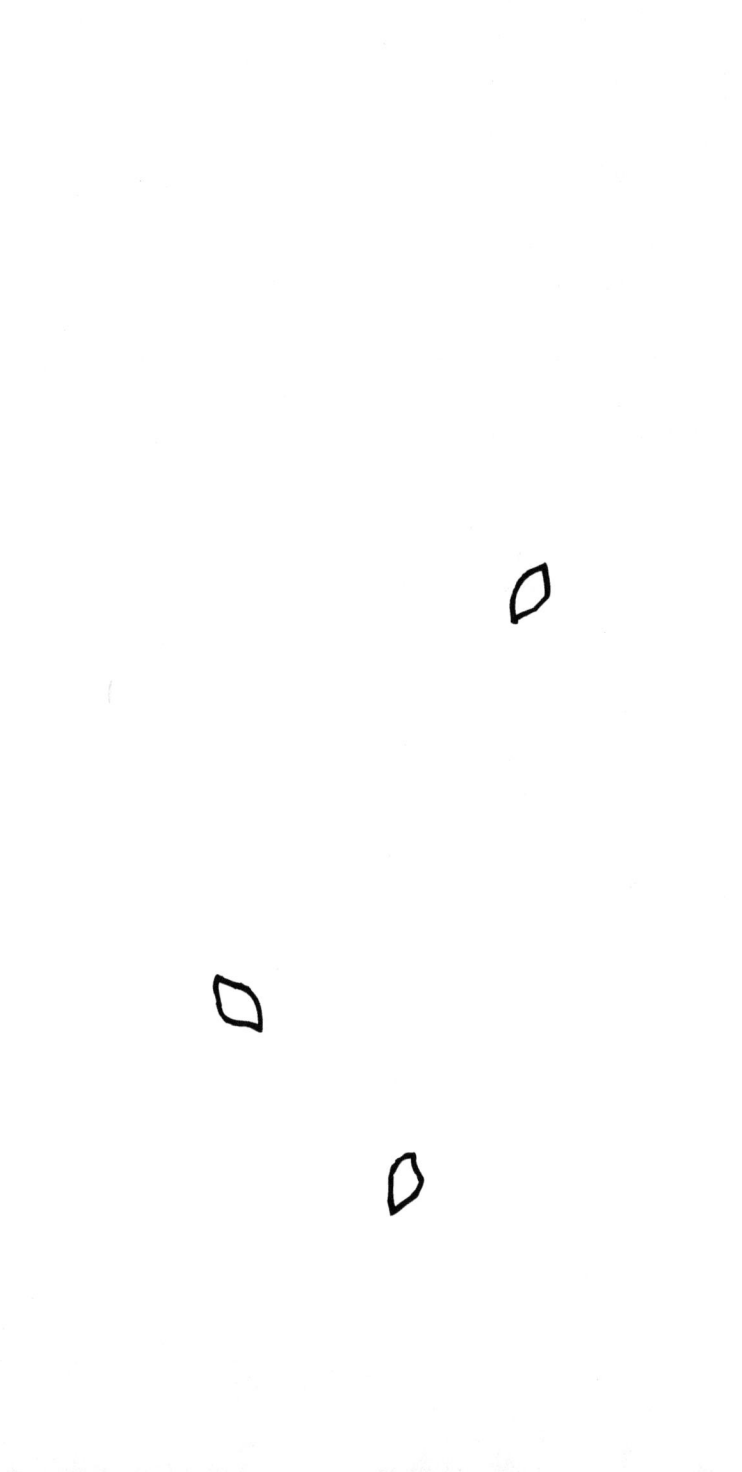

My Mind is Spread

My mind is spread. There is only one but many others that appear then disappear like short British summers.

The heart is messy. And if no one can be, can exist, if he is, then what will become of it? Of my life, of my name? As I slip out of houses into the black night with blood dripping from my shoes.

Stay home. Stay in. Away from them all. Until you let go of that which brews within.

My question is when?

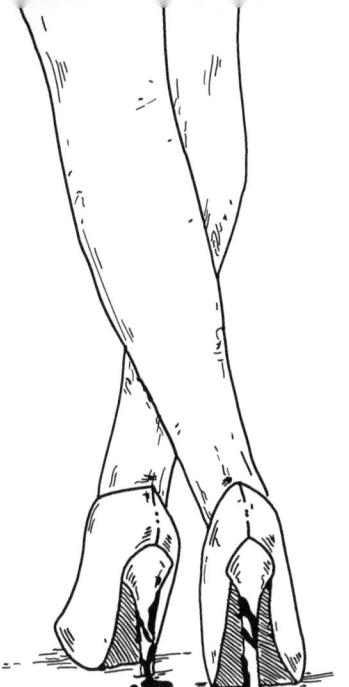

The chaos of longing (K.Y. Robinson)

This is a gush
I've replaced you with poetry
And I am emptying these lines
Like I do this glass

Beautiful sisters
You speak my soul like a song
Cracked my body into movement
Leaking your lines I lingered on

And I am harmful because I go
Back to the chapters that I know
Touch it with my filters
Chase the words with my fingers

I clutch the art to my heart
As I let tears leave me like wishes
You did leave us with epiphany
But I'm afraid longing never left me

Motions and potions

Motions
Potions
My every day lotions

Everyone believes it
Magic and faking it

Every minute
My tears
Hold on, in my sockets
Every day
My fears
Have me repetitive
And lifeless

Motors
Humming
Cloned hearts
Drumming
Stomach turning
Familiarity
Burns me

On the brink
Of rocking
Shaking
Breaking it

Let it be in right mind
Destruction is never kind

Healing

How strange
That beneath the Thai sun
You let the layers of society leave you
Until you were light, arms swinging, and out for embrace

Your bright soul, so whole
And forward-facing did take
My hand, my thoughts, my heart, so fast

I shed a tear for every layer that rejoined you
Attaching itself to your stumbling soul
Then dragging you down, so close to the ground
You thought it easier to succumb to the soil

And now, my memories, fresh like clean grass
Which cut just like glass, and hurt like cold nights
I am still as the night, prayers born of the night
I wonder since when did the sun set so fast?

*

Thinking of you gives me words for years
As the pain eases and the dark clouds of my mind clear
I say time is sweet now, but I must admit my past cursing
It was my greatest challenge, and newest fear

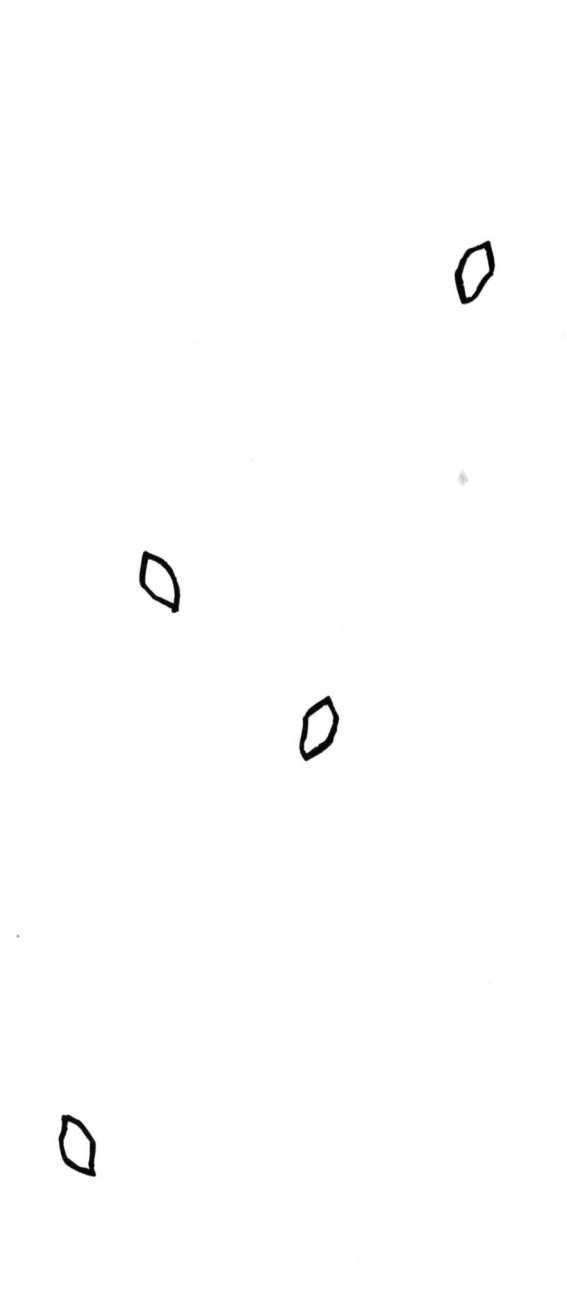

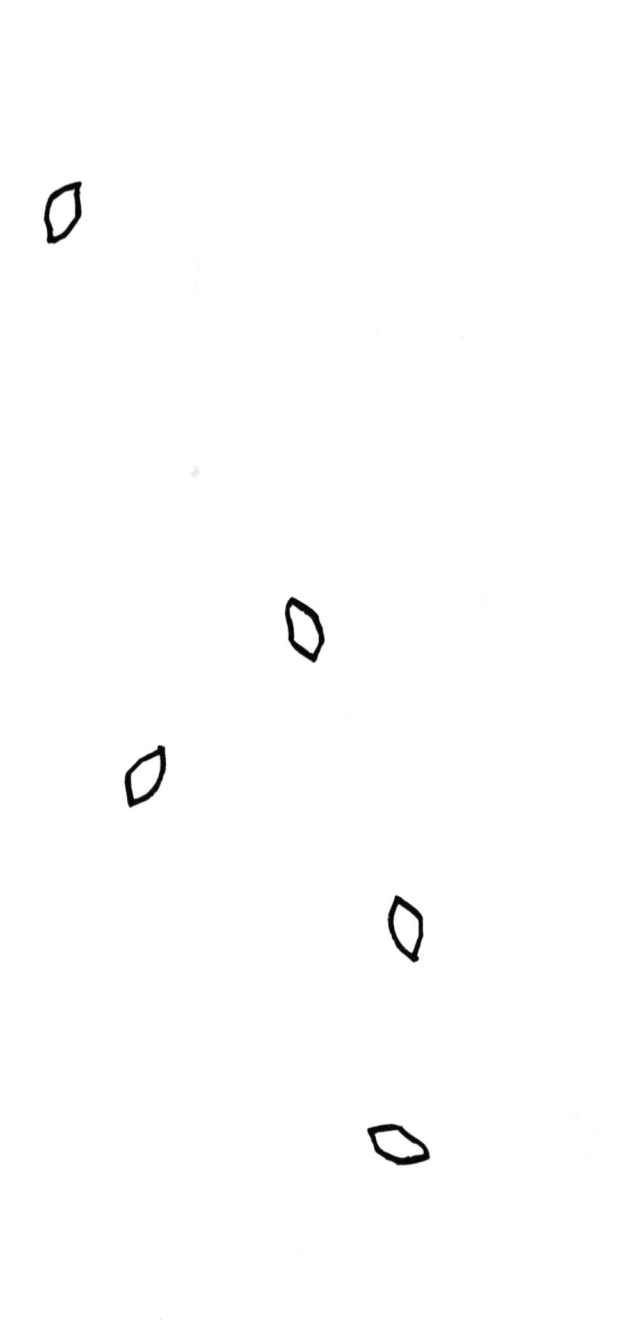

"And now, I have no more words for your ego forever"

Thank you

So you made it to the end? Thank you.

What started off as a little passion project has surely become a mammoth-creative project of which I have to thank some people for offering their good time to me.

Firstly, Grace-Anne Marius - for reading through all the poems, editing and giving me some things to think about. And lastly and most importantly Sinduja Chandrapalan - who has been with me through this entire journey and helped bring my brain musings to life, through the wonderful art of design. Your patience and creativity was truly appreciated, and I hope to work together again in the future.

In this book live 56 poems, plus an essay, but if you would like to view more of my work you can find me on Instagram at @kyomiwade or by searching the hashtag #SadnessAndShortBliss. Nothing would thrill me more than to hear what you thought of the poems, or to see your creative pictures of the book in your home.

It is now that we must say goodbye, but never really. And once again dear reader, I hope that for you, the sadness does not last forever.

All my love,

- Kyomi Wade

Bonus Poem

People say
The night births
Honest thought
If only
Lights warm
Up a blanket sky
We feel safe
But lonely
In the summer
We don't feel
The cold
But the pain
Is immune from
The sun
With a body
Adorned in wants
Stuffed with rich
Foods but empty
How, I wish I
Could skim your
Skin with my
Longing no
Longer will
I enjoy nights
That romanticise
That show my
Solus shadow
The streets are
Soulless and empty

Too so they
Call me their
Friend, I like
It because
It is what I know
Also, I love you
And you know it
It is nauseous
And why must
You be swayed
By relentless
Gushings, all
Of the desires
Travel in circles
Like liquor
Painting a soft
Drink, but it
Always stains
Because it is
Potent, inexcusably
Present but not
Wanted, we are
Meant to be

Notes

Notes

www.ingramcontent.com/pod-product-compliance
Lightning Source LLC
Chambersburg PA
CBHW061331040426
42444CB00011B/2871